The Ultimate Facebook BluePrint 2021

The key to Facebook Ad Success

TABLE OF CONTENT

Introduction 7

What is a Blueprint? 9

Set up Facebook Business Manager: 11

What is a pixel? 15

Set up Facebook Pixel: 17

Set your Metrics / KPis 21

KPI's Glossary 25

How to create a campaign 27

"Killer" Ads tips 29

Testing Campaign & Budget 31

Pro Tips 35

Advertising Strategy 39

Ad Analysis 41

Horizontal Scaling 45

Vertical Scaling 47

Conclusion 49

Sources 51

Introduction

I am Kelly Tamburi, an young E-Commerce Entrepreneur who tried many advertising strategies to sell online items from my website. I spend thousands of pounds to learn Facebook Ads Strategy in order to have fast results and continuous sales. I experienced different techniques to finally end up with a 5 figure monthly income that replaced my 9 to 5 job.

I wrote this book because I want to share my knowledge and to help people like you that want to learn and to take their E-Business to the next level. I am giving you all the tips and tricks that I've learned while using Facebook Ads.

This is a step-by-step guide for people who have an E-commerce or a Dropshipping business and already have some good knowledge of how Facebook Ads Manager works. It works also for beginners as I inserted a quick recap of important steps that you must fully set up before jumping into Facebook Ads Manager.

This guide will explain to you the first step which is how to create a "Testing Campaign" to find out who is your target audience and let Facebook collect data from your pixel. The second part will be how to understand those data and how to analyse, scale and retarget your Ads in order to increase your ROI.

What is a Blueprint?

A Blueprint is a reproduction of the detailed technical plan. A Facebook Blueprint is a detailed Advertising Strategy plan that has been tested and fully functionable.

Facebook Blueprints are often used to test the efficacy of your marketing campaign. As it is a standard Blueprint which means that it can be used for your Ecommerce store if you have your own brand and it can also be used if you are doing drop shipping. The outcome is the same, increase your ROI and continue to grow.

While doing advertising strategy with Facebook it is important to follow an existing plan (Blueprint) in order to have data, sales and indicators that will allow you to scale your business anytime of the year.

Set up Facebook Business Manager:

A quick recap on how to open a Facebook Business Account. There are few things you need to know about Facebook rules. You can only open 2 business accounts per personal account. You can open and manage up to 25 Ad accounts.

Do not create multiple personal "fake" accounts, Facebook will notice and will not allow you to use those personal accounts. To open a business account, Facebook will ask you to verify your ID with your passport or ID card.

From your personal Facebook, create a Facebook Page for your online store. Customers can view what you are selling and even make direct purchase from your Facebook page. Each Ads that you will create will redirect them to your website on your product page with an URL link.

Click on the top right, Create Account. A pop up will show up and ask you to fill in details of your business: name, address, vat number etc.

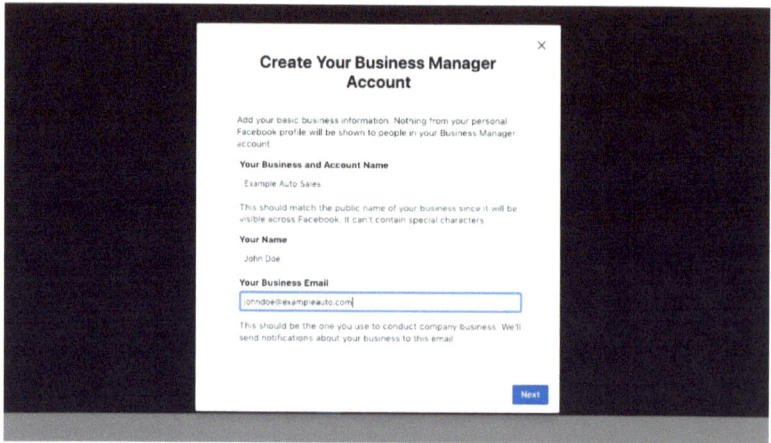

From there you will see your **Business ID** (do not confuse it with your Pixel ID), create an **Ad account**, where you will pay your Ads. For an Ad **Account** I would advise you to connect it to a Credit card rather than a Debit Card as you need to ensure that you will always have funds to pay your Ads. If Facebook can not receive money from you because you do not have funds, Facebook will block your account and it is quite tricky to unblock it.

Connect the **Pixel** to the Ad Account. It should looks like this:

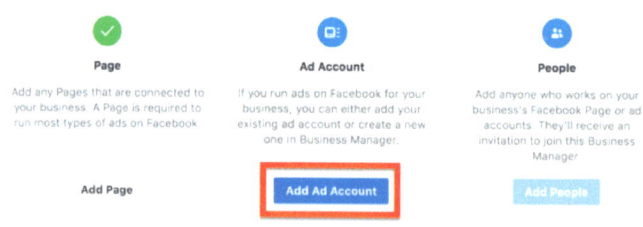

Your **Business ID** is connected to your **Ad Account** which is connected to **Facebook Page** which is connected to your

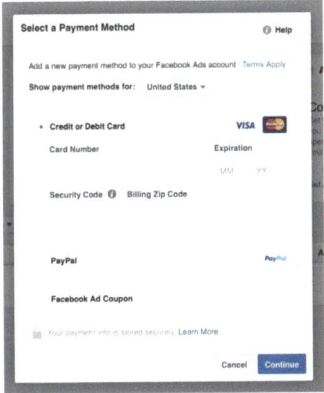

Pixel. Make sure everything is connected before moving further.

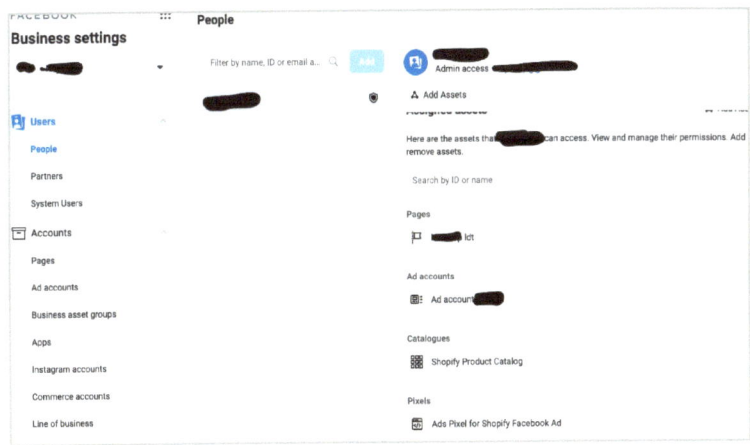

When created, go to Ads Manager. Ads Manager is where you will create your campaign, adset, ads. You will also plan the budget and analyse your ads performance.

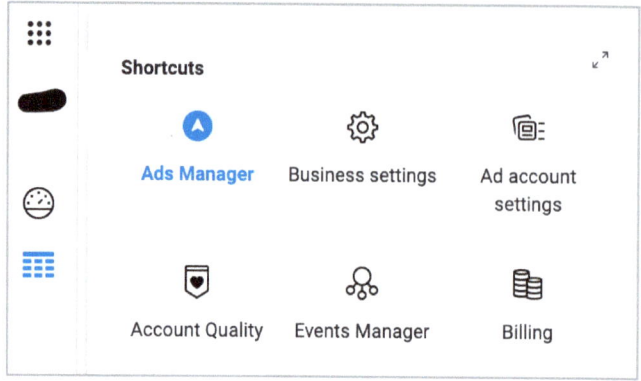

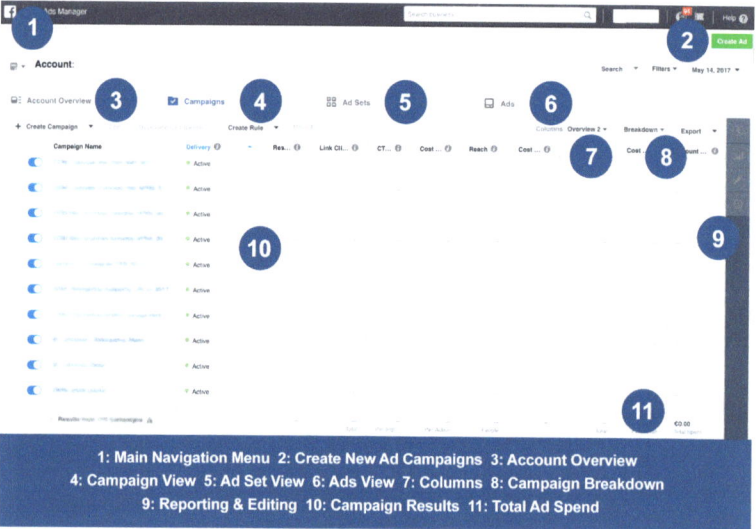

See above the overview of your Facebook Ads Manager. That's the platform you will spend time to create advertising campaigns, analyse your ads performance and increase your ROI.

What is a pixel?

A pixel is what will use Facebook for collecting data. It is important that you set up Facebook pixel on your "Shopify" store before jumping to create a Facebook Business Account.

Facebook is collecting tons of data everyday, when you connect the pixel to your online store, Facebook can give you deep details on what's happening on your website lively and it will save all the information on your Facebook Ads Manager Account when created. **The pixel is the key for Facebook Ads.** Without it, Facebook can't not give you detailed reports on the performance of your Ads. The more your pixel has data, the more is incredibly powerful.

You can not pursue this step-by-step guide **if your Facebook Pixel is not connected to your Shopify Store**. Simply because the Blueprint provides analysis of metrics and actions that need to be taken depending on your data.

Set up Facebook Pixel:

1. Go on Google Chrome and download "Pixel Helper", install it. Pin it on your bookmarks in order to always have easy access to it.

2. Find your Facebook Pixel ID on FAcebook Business Manager. From Ads Manager, click the "Hamburger" Menu icon and select Pixels.

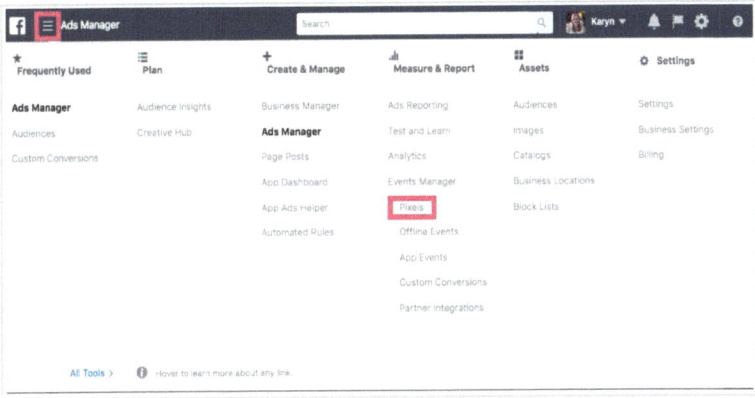

3. Copy your Pixel ID (or click to create a new one if you do not have one already)

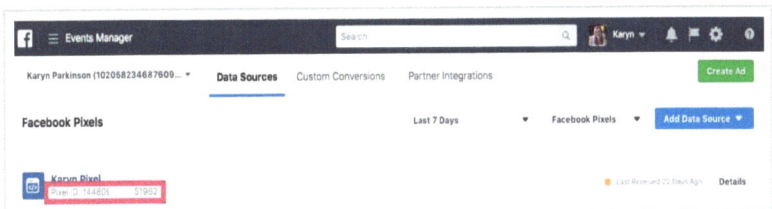

4. Head to your Shopify admin, Select "Online Store" from your Shopify Menu, then Preferences. Scroll down and it will say Facebook Pixel ID, Paste your Facebook pixel ID and save.

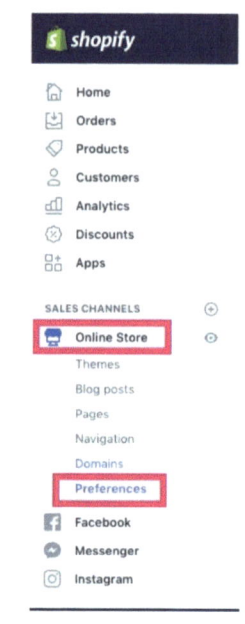

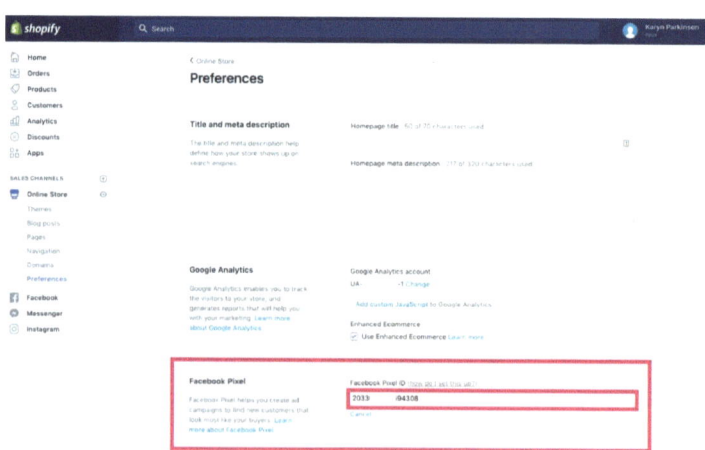

5. Your Facebook pixel is now installed on your Shopify store. When clicking on the eye to view your "Online store", the pixel will automatically be turned on.

6. To check if your pixel is installed correctly, go on your website and Click on "Pixel Helper" icon to see which pixels are firing.

   You should have green ticks for the PageView pixel on every page. Test your pixel when adding a product to cart.

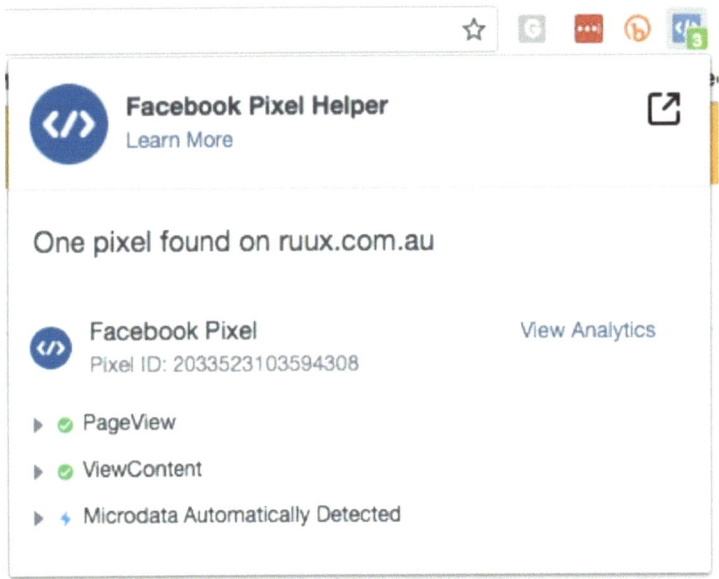

Set your Metrics / KPis

It is important that you understand that Metrics and KPi's have the same meaning, there are both performance indicators. Metrics are mainly used for choosing target audience and KPi's are mainly used for overview on how well your ads went on your "Ads Manager platform".

Metrics in Facebook terms, means indicators. You will find metrics when choosing your target audience for your Ad Sets. Examples of metrics: Interests, Age Group, Gender, Countries, Life Events, Income, demographic.

What is KPis?

Key Performance Indicators are numbers that act as "score" on how your ads wet well. To edit your KPi's columns: Click on Columns:Performance and then click on "Customise Columns".

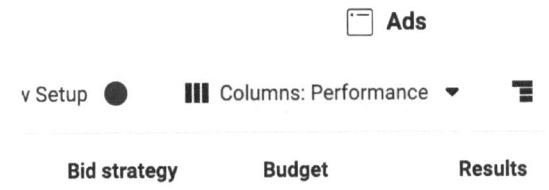

- Performance (Default)
- Setup
- Delivery
- Engagement
- Video Engagement
- App Engagement
- Carousel engagement
- Performance and Clicks
- Cross-device
- Offline conversions
- Targeting and creative
- Bidding and optimisation
- Messenger engagement

Customise Columns...

Set as Default

Reset Column Widths

KPi's list that you should add in your "Customise Columns":

- Name of your campaign
- Name of your Adset
- Amount spent
- Budget
- Add To Cart on the website
- Purchase on the website
- Cost per purchase
- ROAS purchases on the website

- Website - Value of Purchase
- View on landing page
- View on unique content
- Payment from website
- Video watched 25%
- Video watched 50%
- Video watched 75%
- Video watched 95%
- Percentage of video views
- Relevance rating
- Diffusion
- Interaction with your ads
- Interaction with your page
- AOV
- LTV
- UATC
- UIC
- OUTBOUND CLICK
- ROAS
- CAC
- CTR (LINK)
- CPM
- PVC
- ULPV
- UCPLV

KPI's Glossary:

AOV
Average Order Value - The average amount spent per purchase.

LTV
Lifetime Value - The total value spent across a customer's life.

UATC
Unique Add To Cart - The first step in the checkout process.

UIC
Unique Initiate Check Out - The second step in the checkout process.

Outbound Click
Clicks that take you off of Facebook owned properties.

ROAS
Return On Ad Spend - The money you receive derived from spending on advertising.

CAC
Cost of Acquiring a Customer - The amount of dollars spent to convince a consumer to buy your product.

CTR (Link)
Click Through Rate (Link) - The % of times people who saw and clicked on your link.

CPM

Cost Per 1000 Impressions - The cost to deliver our ad for 1000 impressions.

PCV

Purchase Conversion Value - The revenue seen from Facebook specific purchases.

ULPV

Unique Landing Page View - The number of consumers who made it to your landing page.

UCPLV

Unique Cost Per Landing Page View - The average cost per each landing page visit.

How to create a campaign:

Go on Facebook Ads manager, you will see the view of your campaign, empty if you just started, filled in if your already created campaigns. Click on the left green button; "Create Campaign".

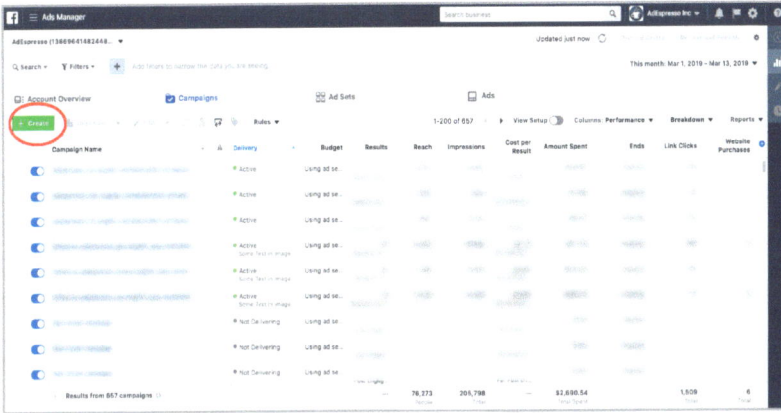

Aim of your campaign: "**Conversion**" always, choose a name for your Campaign, Create Adset (group of Ads where you can specify target audience, budget etc), Create your Ads (Your Creative).

I would advise you and will explain it better below how to create 2 campaigns, 1 CBO and 1 ABO. You can name them like this so you will not be confused: "Campaign Shampoo CBO" & "Campaign Shampoo ABO".

Use 3-5 different creative (Videos, Photos) per Ad Sets. Change the thumbnails of each Creative, you can keep the same Ad Copy for all ads.

"Killer" Ads tips

Ad Creative: Photo ads. Use HIGH QUALITY photos and videos. But it's better if you use videos you will have more interaction with your customer. If using videos remember to add text (feature, benefits) because many customers do not listen to the Ad just watched it.

The first 3 sec are crucial, show your product in action, product results, zoom on your product or zoom on the main product's feature. Use flashy colours for your thumbnails, big text in uppercase and use emojis.

Show clearly your promo code is uppercase and bold text. Make your promo code easy to remember. For example: **PROMO CODE: BOWL20**

Ad Copy: Keep the Ad Copy simple. Have a simple sentence highlighting benefits and use emojis. It is important to put in your description if you are offering Free Shipping.

Example of Ad Copy for any kind of products, you can edit to your brand name and requirements

Text 1: YOUR NEW MORNING ROUTINE

Text 2: Remove blackheads, grease, acne, dirt, whiteheads, dead skin

        Eliminate pores

Soft and Smooth Skin

24 H   Limited Offer   50%OFF
Free Shipping   Get Yours TODAY

Headline example 1 :   SOP SPENDING MONEY ON SKINCARE TREATMENT

Headline example 2:   4.9/5 - GET YOURS TODAY

Testing Campaign & Budget

Why is the testing phase important for your first campaign?

Testing phase is crucial at the beginning of your advertising strategy because you do not have data. You need to test your product as soon as possible to check if it is a winning product, see how your ads perform and understand who will be your potential customers. You need to collect data to understand your target audience and then retarget and scale your business.

Some data are so specific that you can create "saved audiences" for future campaigns to retarget only recurrent customers (Customers that bought at least 1 items on your store).

To reach new customers that will depend on your first testing, how well it was and from there you can use the same audience and add under Behavior (metrics) **"Engaged shopper"** (Shoppers that bought an item online the last few days).

This phase will give you deep details on where your future customers are (demographic). I would advise you to choose one market per campaign for the testing phase. Popular markets are: USA, FRANCE, UK, CANADA, AUSTRALIA. The market most used by many dropshipper is the USA because there is a huge population that buys online.

Below you have 2 different testing plans for your campaign. It is important to always set the aim to **"Conversion"** and make sure the pixel is connected to: **green** bullet point **"purchase"**.

If you are about to create a new campaign and if you are not seeing your pixel in green, you need to go to your "Shopify" store, under promotion, create a 100% voucher, buy your items (00.00$) and then your pixel will record the purchase. Go back to your Facebook Ads Manager, refresh the page and continue to create your campaign, check the "pixel helper", it should be in green.

I would advise you to do 2 Testing Campaign, one with CBO and one with ABO in order to increase your ROAS and collection of data.

CBO stands for Campaign Budget optimization which means that it automatically manages your campaign budget across Ad Sets to get the best results. With CBO you set one central campaign budget. Facebook's Algorithms will use your budget accordingly through your campaign in real time and will give you the best opportunities. CBO testing method is known to provide performance and value gains across campaigns.

Testing method CBO (Campaign Optimization) - Turn it on
- Aim: Conversion (Always)
- Budget: £120 per day

- Adset: 3-5 Ad Sets maximum (3-5 creative per Ad Set)
- Target Audience: 3 interests + 2 broads (target without interests)
- Audience size: 1M to 10M minimum or more if you have data
- Placement: Always in automatic placement
- Age: 18+

ABO stands for Ad Set Budget Optimization, you simply allocate a budget to Ad sets and manage each Ad set's budget individually. ABO method allows you to know earlier whether that campaign will perform or not. ABO is also often used after the testing phase when you decide to retarget a campaign as it gives more control over the spending of each audience group.

Testing method ABO (Normal campaign) - Turn it on
- Aim: Conversion (Always)
- Budget: £120 per day
- Adset: define the number of Ad set / your daily budget / AOV = 4 Ad sets - (3-5 creative per Ad Set)
- Target audience: 3 interests + 2 broads (target without interests)
- Audience size: 1M to 10M minimum or more if you have data
- Placement: Always in automatic placement
- Age: 18+

If you have a small budget, but want results you would need to put a minimum of £100 for your campaigns (£50 - Campaign CBO & £50 - Campaign ABO). For the Testing campaign let it for at least 3 days in order to let Facebook's Algorithm do the work and collect data.

Pro Tips

Below you will find a list of my "Pro Tips" that helps me to scale my business by understanding the tricks for creating ads, campaigns, websites in order to increase profits.

- One of your Ad Set - interests set it to "UPCOMING BIRTHDAY"

- If Beauty/Cosmetics products, use FEMALE only for Gender

- Always in CONVERSION, Optimization "PURCHASE" (Pixel must be green)

- If Dropshipper does not use in your Ads (Creative) with Before and After pictures or videos, Facebook does not accept it and Facebook could block your account.

- On your online store add UGC (User-Generated-Content), photos of existing customers using your product. It can be pictures from reviews. By adding some pictures to your store on your homepage, potential customers will identify themself to them and would most likely purchase your product.

    If you work with influencers that help to, repost their picture on your social media (FAcebook/Instagram) and always have the CTA (Call-to-Action) button, "Shop Now".

- Your thumbnail should not have more than 20% of text if it is more than this, Facebook Ads will refuse your Ad.

- When choosing Broad interest for your campaign it is simply a general and not specific interest, for example: Beauty, Health, Fitness, Cooking…

- Use the same pixel if you have a second boutique related to your first boutique. For example if your first boutique is selling yoga mats, you can use the same pixel for the second store which is selling fitness equipment.

- For your creative (Ads), use emotions words, pictures and videos depending on your product. For example as a thumbnail with a woman smiling because of a new pillow that reduces her neck pain will increase your chance to attract more customers clicking on your ad.

- Use GIF on your website in your product page under product description. Customers want to know how to use the product before making a decision. Add 2-3 GIF on main features of your products and it will increase trust between your and your potential future buyers.

- Make sure that all your CTA's are correctly linked to your product page. Make the steps easier for your customers. Watch Ad > Swipe Up to Shop Now > Product page link > Buy Now / Add to Cart > Make payment.

For my online store which has only 1 main product, I delete the option of "Add to Cart", I made sure that my Ads are very clear (Video of how to use the product) and when customer swipe up to shop now, he lands on the product page, have a clear picture of the product with the CTA (Call to Action): BUY NOW. From BUY NOW, it jumps directly to the checkout and asks the method of payment. Personally it works well for my store, I would advise you to try it out only if you have a website selling 1 main product.

Advertising Strategy

Apply this strategy only if you already did a Campaign with ABO and CBO in the last 3 days. If not stick to **ABO/CBO** until you have **at least 1 purchase**.

Ad objective: Test a website **"Conversion"** and optimized for **"Purchase"** always.

Ages: 18+ (Unless Product can be tailored to lower audience margin range).

Countries: This list should be saved in your country's locations on Ads.
- Belgium
- Italy
- United Kingdom
- Denmark
- Finland
- Czech Republic
- Ireland
- Sweden
- Switzerland
- Poland
- Greece
- United States
- Spain
- Netherlands
- Norway
- France

- Australia
- Canada
- New Zealand
- Germany

Detailed Targeting: Less is more. Keep it related to what you are selling & use 1 interest per ad set. For example, let's say you are selling a dog collar. Use large audience interests (1m+) eg. Dogs, Dog walking, Pets, Dog Lover, Dog equipment.

Don't use super small interests eg. Pitbull lover magazine (3,000 audience). The higher your audience, the cheaper your ads will be delivered + the more broad of an audience Facebook has to choose purchasers from. I tend to look for my Ad set audience to be around 1m-20m.

Exclude Targeting: Shopify, Aliexpress, Drop Shipping, Ecommerce. (So competitors don't see your ads).

Device: Mobile Only

Placements: Instagram Feed Only (ATC Starting), Feed & Stories (When Ads Start To Work and you move to optimize for PUR)

Conversion Window: 7 day Click/ 1-day view optimisation

Ad Analysis

After Testing your product with the Testing Campaign ABO/CBO, it's time to analyse how well your ads performed and which action you should take to scale your business.

Never delete campaigns with Adsets and Ads before analysing them because your Kpi's results are crucial and tell you what is doing well and what is doing wrong. It can also show you if there is a problem in your creative (ads) or something wrong on your website. Each data and score are important.

With PUR (Purchase) optimization (Pixel) - You are looking for sales. Always look at the current day when your testing (TODAY) - If you are scaling you look at the last 4 days.

Metrics (Always known as KPI) to look for, 1-2 days after launch:

High Relevance Score: Higher than 7

High Cost Per ATC? Low CPC?: Overall your site is the problem. People clicked your Ad because they were interested. Something turned them away.

High Cost Per Click/High ATC (Add To Cart)/ Low Relevance Score?: You Ad Creative is the problem. Change your image (most important) or Ad Copy.

When trying to lower the CPC (Cost Per Click), or ATC (Add to Cart) cost, try and come up with better Ad Copies that can resonate with your audience.

(You want below $1 but may have to tweak anything between $1-$2 that's consistent or becomes cheaper. Usually your CP-ATC = 5x CPP (Cost Per Purchase).

Low/Medium ATC? High CPC? High Relevance Score?: Work on a better audience. Maybe your audience is not the best.

No Purchase?: If you don't see purchases after 1-2 days. Kill it. Start over with a new product & repeat the process. (Search and Choose Winning products).

Day 2: if relevancy score is under 7 but all the metrics/KPI's are good, change the Ad Copy, change to a new picture or video. But make sure you're optimizing for Purchase (pixel) since you already vetted the product in ATC so it definitely works.

If your CPC was good and CP-ATC was under $2 or $1 depending on the country, then duplicate the good Ad Sets and make the ad to optimize for purchase (pixel).

If most of our ATC Ads are having really good metrics/KPi's, (Cheap CPC and Cheap ATC), then that's when you start duplicating those into purchase ads.

Once those are starting, show some traction and that they work, on day 1 or 2, then you know it's a winning product where you can test all aspects for.

Horizontal Scaling

Horizontal scaling is one of the most popular methods to scale Facebook campaigns and it is widely used. With this technique, you duplicate the same winning Ads but target them to a different audience.

Create new Ad Sets and reuse the same ads (creative). Find a new audience that you can scale to a decent point, before you move onto another audience and see what else works.

If CPC is Good, Relevance Score BAD, ATC is Trash = Customer sees product and likes it that's why ATC is bad, therefore it has to be something with the website.

Once you start to optimize for purchase (pixel) after all the ATC Ads have shown good metrics/KPi's and traction, that's when you TEST TEST TEST.

Here we test all the "Interests". If it's girly product (e.g. cosmetics, beauty products) we can test thing like:
- Kim Kardashian
- MAC Cosmetics
- Rihanna
- Competitors
- Engaged Shoppers with no interest
- The stuff above with engaged shoppers
- Country with engaged shoppers
- Different age ranges for all the above
- Country by themselves

When testing multiple variables, Test different thumbnails (product in action, customer reviews, customers emotions), and videos.

Test USA separately if a good amount of traffic is coming from there. If the metrics/KPi's for Feed Ads are looking good, test for Story too.

Budget: When you start to have 3 or 5 Ad sets that are performing AMAZING, then simply use the edit tool from the ads manager over the budget columns and you can increase the budget. THIS DOES NOT RUN THE OPTIMIZATION FOR THE AD. However sometimes it takes about a day to restart to optimize.

Horizontal Scaling allows you to have smaller budget Adsets. You can create new ad sets with a minimum of £30 with the same ads (Creative).

Example: $30 Ad Set with good metrics/KPi's, has been getting some sales, you increase to $45, from there is that performs well increase to $50, then $75, and then $100.

Duplicate all winning IG carousel Ads to Facebook carousel Ads. 90% chance of it working.

Vertical Scaling

Vertical scaling is the most popular and straightforward growth strategy that you can apply for your campaigns. This is the scaling method that works the best for me and has incredible numbers after 1-2 days.

When you scale vertically, you simply increase the budget on your existing campaigns and on Ad sets to reach more customers. It really increases the audience that can be reached, the more money you add, the more people you reach and the more new data is stored. Simply duplicate your one or two winning ad sets and increase the budgets.

How to do it:

1 Ad set - set to £100 for 1 day
2nd Ad set - set to £100 for 1 day

If an adset has consistently been making profits and having good metrics/KPi's, you can vertical scale and increase budget accordingly and saved audiences.

Conclusion

It is important to test your products over 3 days before scaling or retargeting. Have a winning product from start in order to focus on the Testing Campaign Phase then Analysis and Level up. Remember to save your winning audience to re-used it later for future campaigns.

To conclude, I hope this Facebook Blueprint gives you the knowledge and an Action Plan for your online business. After that, you are free to try different audiences, budgets and either to try different advertising strategies.

Sources

https://fitsmallbusiness.com/how-to-facebook-pixel-helper/
https://chrome.google.com/webstore/detail/facebook-pixel-helper/fdgfkebogiimcoedlicjlajpkdmockpc
https://karynwithay.com/how-to-install-the-facebook-pixel-on-shopify/
https://blog.hootsuite.com/fr/facebook-business-manager/
https://9clouds.com/blog/how-to-set-up-facebook-business-manager/
https://www.socialmediatoday.com/news/facebook-abandons-mandatory-shift-to-campaign-budget-optimization-for-ad-ca/576490/
https://dimniko.com/blog/when-to-use-abo-and-cbo/
https://www.jeero.co/ecommerce-u/campaign-budget-optimization-guide
https://adespresso.com/guides/facebook-ads-beginner/setting-up-your-facebook-ads-account/
https://www.socialmediaexaminer.com/how-to-create-facebook-ad-with-business-manager/
https://adespresso.com/guides/facebook-ads-beginner/facebook-manager-campaign-setup/

www.ingramcontent.com/pod-product-compliance
Lightning Source LLC
Chambersburg PA
CBHW040244220526
45473CB00001B/360